Sermon Series 18S
(For All Occasions)

Sermon Outlines For Easy Preaching

Dr. Joseph R. Rogers, Sr.

Introduction

The Preaching of the gospel is a great opportunity to share with the people of God some wonderful and enriching insights. The word **'PREACH'** means to lecture, to sermonize, to speak or to deliver the message of the Lord Jesus Christ.

The bible speaks loud, clear and with authority as it relates **who must preach** and the **reason for preaching (teaching).** The Apostle Paul writes to the Romans in chapter ten and said, [15] And how shall they preach, except they be sent? as it is written, How beautiful are the feet of them that preach the gospel of peace, and bring glad tidings of good things!

Why must the gospel be preached? The Apostle Paul writes again to the church a Corinth and said, "*But if our gospel be hid, it is hid to them that are lost.*" (2 Corinthians 4:3) So, the

2

Lord Jesus Christ need lips of clay to deliver His message to the lost, as well as to the believer's for growth, strength and development.

It is my pray that you will find these short outlines helpful as you go into your secret closet (prayer and study time) and seek the Lord's guidance as you prepare for those whom He has commissioned you to led.

Whatever you do take preaching serious, look at the ministry with all seriousness—in doing so the Lord will richly bless your efforts as you yield your members the Holy Ghost.

Be Blessed And Preach The Gospel!
Joseph R. Rogers, Sr., D. Min.

Table Of Contents

Page No.

4

The Devil's Brew Is Dirty Business
A Sermon By Dr. Joseph R. Rogers, Sr.
For The Greater Philadelphia Church
Raleigh, North Carolina 27603
Theme: Spiritual Drunkenness
March 13, 2011

Scripture: "Look not thou upon the "WINE" when it is 'RED', when it giveth his color in the cup, when it moveth itself alright. At the last it biteth like a "Serpent", and stingeth like and "Adder". (Proverbs 23:31, 32) (Read Proverbs 23:17-35)

Introduction
There has been much debate in the classroom of Seminaries, Divinity Schools and Bible Colleges as is relates to the intake of **"intoxicating beverages"**. There are those who say that it is all-right as long as you do not get DRUNK.

There are also those who say that a little wine for the stomach sakes (Paul's advice to Timothy) is all right with the Lord. There are those who say that I rather deal with those who drink than to deal with liars, back bitter...etc.

Well, my brothers and sisters what you think, what I think and the opinion of others do not count; it is what the Word of God says that "is" the difference. It is ashamed for anyone who *knows* the Lord to condone the consumption of drinks that will cause a person to lose their control (Read Church Covenant).

I am fully aware that people in those towns, which make this joy juice, have to earn their living. In the *"Good Life City" Miller's Brewery.* Before Miller's Brewery ever arrived, there was Viking Distillery, which is, I think Georgia's first legalized distillery. There is Albany Beverage Company, along with many others, who produce and sell alcohol.

Most Christian people that I know and I hope Philadelphia Baptist Church are against alcohol consumption as an intoxicating beverage.

I just want to remind us all of how DEVILISH the "Devil's Brew" really "IS". I am afraid if things are not *'checked'* that we are in danger of getting use to the presence of liquor in this area that we don't cry against it as a sin anymore.

I call it the *devil's brew* because it is like a "SERPENT", and it gives "HIS color' (the reference was to the red color of wine, and the devil's color as a serpent is red) in the cup.

Exposition I
I. THE DEVIL'S BREW "DERIDES":
(Makes a "Fool" Out of You)
Proverbs 20:1-"Wine is a mocker, strong drink is raging: and whosoever is deceived thereby is not wise".

What does it do to one that partakes? Damage!! Damage!!

It makes you "talk" foolishly.
It makes you "think" foolishly.
It makes you "toil foolishly" -- living for the next drink, the next paycheck to spend at the bar.

II. THE DEVIL'S BREW "DELUDES":
(Deceives; Betrays You)
Isaiah 28:7"But they also have "erred" through wine, and through strong drink are out of the way; the "priest" and the "prophet" have "erred" through strong drink, they are swallowed up of wine, they are "out of the way" through strong drink; they err in vision, they "stumble" in judgment.

A man or woman of God should never "condone' the consumption of alcohol beverages for intoxicating. I remember embarrassing a preacher one time many years ago by catching him at a grocery store cashier line with a six-pack of beer in front of him.

One of the problems with today's society with regard to booze and other social evils is that there are just too many compromising, politicking, pussy-footing, ear-scratching, man-pleasing, lily-livered, beauty parlor & barber shop SPEAKERS, which refuse to take a STAND!!.

As people of God we should that attitude of devil-hating, sin-killing, hell-fire, Christ-exalting, GOD-fearing, Bible-believing & saints enforcing who will cry against sin!!!)

The Devil's Brew:
It deceives preachers - they won't preach against it.

It deceives politicians - they are bought by it.

It deceives peoples - they think it is necessary.

Exposition II
III. THE DEVIL'S BREW "DEFILES":
(Violates; Corrupts)
Proverbs 23:33-"Thine eyes shall behold strange women, and thine heart shall utter perverse things".

- It defiles your "mind".
- It defiles your "mouth".
- It defiles your "morals".

IV. THE DEVIL'S BREW DESTROYS:
(Kills Futures, Visions)
Proverbs 23:32-"At the last it biteth like a serpent, and stingeth like an adder.

- It destroys one's "home".
- It destroys one's "health".
- It destroys one's "hope".

V. THE DEVIL'S BREW DRAINS:
(Exhaust)
Proverbs 23:21-"For the drunkard and the glutton shall come to poverty: and drowsiness shall clothe a man with rags.

- Your "checking account"
- Your "children"
- Your "character"

VI. THE DEVIL'S BREW "DEADENS": (Stops You From Achieving)

Proverbs 23:35a-" They have stricken me, shalt thou say, and I was not sick; they have beaten me, and I felt it not...etc."

- Your "conscience".
- Your "concern".
- Your 'consciousness".

VII. THE DEVIL'S BREW DOMINATES: (Takes Control)

Proverbs 23:35b-"... when shall I awake? I will seek it yet again.

It dominates the fool who takes it.
It dominates the family affected by it.
It dominates the future of those hooked on it.

Conclusion

So, as I close this message the text says, "Look not thou upon the *"WINE"* when it is 'RED', when it giveth his color in the cup, when it moveth itself alright. At the last it biteth like a "Serpent", and stingeth like and "Adder".
`

I am happy to announce that every one have not gone to the dogs. There are some righteous folks who "love" the Lord and "abiding" in His Will. There are those who are not and will not take down— We will fight the good fight of Faith!!

So, *be not "drunk" with wine in excess, but be "filled" with the Spirit (The Spirit Of God)*. When you are filled with the Spirit your business with go right, your relationships will go right, your family life will go right, your marriage will god right.

But most of all you will have a wholesome, fruitful, and joyful relationship with the Lord Jesus Christ. Do not respond like Noah. He got drunk and...

Uncovered His Nakedness,
Embarrassed His Family,
Damaged His Integrity,
Ruined His Character,
"The Devil's Brew Is Dirty Business"
Joseph R. Rogers, Sr., D. Min.
Pastor/Teacher

A True Friend

A Sermon By Dr. Joseph R. Rogers, Sr.
For The Greater Philadelphia Church
Raleigh, North Carolina 27603
Theme: True Friends
March 6, 2011

Scripture: "Greater love hath no man than this, that a man lay down his life for his friends". **(St. John 15:13)**

Introduction

My brothers and sisters, God has made every individual different in physicality, personality, likes, dislikes was well and spiritual gifts and talents. In that we are different and independent; yet we are also interdependent.

Which is to say, even though we are individualistic in nature; yet we need companionship and friendship to be balanced in development and application. Remember, no man is an island and no man stands alone.

True Friends are rarities but so called friends come by the basket full and a dime a dozen. In today's society, we should be very selective about those persons whom we choose to call our friends.

We should be careful because the terms 'friend' mean different things to different people. To some a friend is someone who agrees with them and they control their lives. A True Friend is someone who is supported whether you're right or wrong and has your welfare and the top of this list.

Now, Webster defines a friend as companion, buddy or pal. Being a true friend is both an honor and a privilege. A friend is more than a neighbor. A friend sticks closer than a brother or sister, not the drain you dry or use you as a puppet:

- A True Friend tells us the truth.
- A True Friend warns us of danger.
- A True Friend does not condone our wrong doing.

A True Friend expresses their friendship much the same as David and Jonathan did. True friends are an invaluable asset. There are a few levels that must be achieved before a person

fills the role as **"True Friend"**. The bible says, *"A man that hath friends must* *shew himself friendly: and there is a friend that sticketh closer than a brother"*.

In our lives we will be face with three (3) of people for different reasons, but when the dust settles God will work all things out for our good.

1. COMRADES - *These are people who are against what you are against.* Don't make the mistake of thinking these people are for you - they're not. They aren't even for what you are for. They are simply against what you are against. These folks are fighters and if you don't direct your fighting in the direction that they desire they will ultimately fight against you.

2. CONSTITUENTS - *These are people who are for what you are for.* Don't make the mistake of thinking that these people are for you. They aren't. They are for what you are for and when that commonality ends, constituents will no longer be for you at all.

3. CONFIDANTS - *These are people who are for you.* They are for you in the good times and the bad times. They are for you because you are you. If you find three

people like this in your lifetime, you
are blessed.

Exposition I

As Christians, we rejoice in knowing
that we have a friend in Jesus and He
always loves us. He will always be for
us, with us; and he will never leave us
alone. Today, remember that Jesus is your
True Friend.

- He will never let you down.
- He will always love you.
- He will not change His love
  when you are wrong.
- He has you back.
- He will not tell your business

The bible says, "No greater love can
a person show for another than his
willingness to lay down his life in his
defense (Help. Admonish)".

For Jesus this meant the ultimate
sacrifice. It meant his death on Calvary
to provide a means for the men and women
of this world to have eternal life and
forgiveness of sin.

- ➤ A True Friend will make sacrifices of their time.
- ➤ A True Friend will go the last mile for others.
- ➤ A True Friend will be there when you need them.

Conclusion

So as I close this message, I am glad to know that True Friends are supportive, instructive, loving (tough love) and encouraging.

A True Friend looks for the right moment and right way to remind their friends, that it doesn't profit a man anything if he gains the whole world and loses his soul!

A True Friend who knows what true friendship entails: In St. John 15:15 Jesus said, *"Henceforth I call you not servants, for the servant knoweth not what his Lord doeth: but I have called you friends."*

What a friend we have in Jesus, for when we have fallen down, he picks us up and turns us around!

What a friend we have in Jesus, when we have dropped our heads in despair, he dries our weeping eyes!

What a friend we have in Jesus, when we feel abandoned, he promises never to leave us. Never to leave us alone!

What a friend we have in Jesus, who showed us the greatest love, when humanity was doomed to an eternal HELL, Jesus Christ paid the ransom for our deliverance.

That why again, A True Friend can say with conviction, *"No greater love can a man show than this, that he would lay down his life for his friends*!

"A True Friend"
Joseph R. Rogers, Sr., D. Min.
Pastor/Teacher

"He's A n On Time God"

A Dr. Joseph R. Rogers, Sr.
For Greater Philadelphia Church
Raleigh, North Carolina 27610
Theme: Time Is Priceless
March 13, 2011

Scripture:"The righteous cry (believers) and the Lord heareth and delivereth them out of their troubles (17)...Many are the afflictions (problems) of the righteous, but the Lord delivereth (saves) him out of them all." (Psalms 34:17, 19)

Introduction

In this wonder text can be use to encourage anyone in their times and moments of "challenge". Just to hear, *"...deliverth them out of them all"*, is certainly "refreshing" and "encouraging".

So in that vein that the Lord wants to assure you and I today that He has not forgotten us and that He will never leave us in the times of great decision—He Is An On Time God!

But who better understood, knew and experienced this than King David:

God delivered his from the sword of King Saul!

God delivered him from the Paw of the Bear and the Mouth of Lion!

God delivered him from the crime of premeditative murder!

God delivered him from the shame act of adultery!

This is how Psalm 51 can into being when he said, [10] "Create in me a clean heart, O God; and renew a right spirit within me. [11] Cast me not away from thy presence; and take not thy holy spirit from me. [12] Restore unto me the joy of thy salvation; and uphold me with thy free spirit".

As God delivered King David in his time of adversity, challenge and trouble; don't you know He will do the same for you and me—He Is An On Time God!

There are a multitude of delivery services across the country, each of which promotes itself as the fastest and the most efficient.

The United States Postal Service or USPS is the only mail delivery service in the country. It can deliver a letter postmarked correctly in two days.

United Parcel Service or UPS, has a network of stations and delivery methods that span the nation, it can deliver a package in 24 hours right to your front door.

Federal Express and Airborne is two express mail companies that promote the fact that they can deliver your package anywhere, over night.

The Western Union can send a message or cash anywhere in the world in a matter of minutes.

These systems offer a fast delivery. They are usually efficient, but even the best of their delivers can be late every now and then.

- USPS mailman runs late.
- UPS trucks break down.
- Western Union computers get bugged.
- Federal Express gets snowed in.

Today, we should take **"joy"** in knowing that we serve a God who is in the blessing business and he can deliver on time! And there is nothing that can stop Him! Whatever you need, God's got it. And He is able to give unto all of us exceedingly abundantly above all that we could think or ask

Exposition I

Our text first considers King David as he writes of his deliverance from his enemies. It is a reference to David's flight from Saul that is recorded in 1 Samuel 21.

Kings David was sustained in his flight by eating the "showbread" or what we might describe as the "communion bread. He eventually escaped his pursuers and was delivered.

Then King David sat down to pen this 34th Psalm, under the inspiration of God, and praised God for delivering him. So should we 'praise' God and thank Him for His goodness.

In verse 17 David uses three words to describe the entire thought of the 34th Psalm, "Cry", "Heareth" and "Delivereth". THE LORD HEARS OUR CRY:

- Our cry can be a deliverance from impending troubles.
- Our cry can be an exclamatory expression of relief!
- Our cry can be a yearning for peace,
- Our cry can be a desire for rest, and
- Our cry can be a hope of better times.

Yes we will CRY as:

Jeremiah cried so much that it took a whole book to contain his lamentations! (Book of Lamentations)

Judah cried so much over Jerusalem's demise that the wall where they prayed was renamed the Wailing Wall!

Yes we cry sometimes, but when you cry, don't cry in self pity but cry out to the Lord!

David said, "I will "lift up mine eyes unto the hills from whence cometh my help, my help cometh from the Lord, who made the heaven and the earth."

Dr. Watts said, "Father I stretch my hands to thee, no other help I know, if thou withdraw thyself from me, whither shall I go!"

Conclusion

So, as I close this message, I am delighted to "know" the God of the Bible and that He is an on time God.

Yes! The righteous cry and the Lord heareth and delivereth them out of their troubles (17)...Many are the afflictions (problems) of the righteous, but the Lord delivereth (saves) him out of them all

The text assures me that we will have trials and tribulation. But, is also confirms to me that it is wonderful to know that in the time of troubles the

Lord has promised to 'hide' us in His pavilion; in the secret places of His tabernacle.

Let me give us some witnesses that have attested to the fact that the Lord Is An On Time God.

Three Hebrew Boys declared that God is able to deliver us from the flames of the fiery furnace!

The Prophet Ezekiel declared God is able to deliver us from the despair of a valley of dry bones.

A Widow woman declared, God is able to keep my barrel from running dry!

A Blind man declared God able to turn darkness of life's journey into sunlight of the goodness of His glory.

A Lame man declared, God is able to raise you up from your bed of affliction.

Yes! He's able to deliver, just in the nick of time." "He may not come when you want, but he's right on time."

Man's delivery has <u>time</u> limitations—
--but our God can deliver anywhere and
anytime. All we have to do is, "Call Him,
Call, and tell him what we want!

Man's delivery has <u>address</u>
limitations: Without the proper address
the postal service will return your
letter marked, "return to sender address
unknown---But God can deliver anywhere
because He knows every address.

He can deliver in California and New
York!

He can deliver in Detroit and New
Orleans!

He can deliver around the world.

God can deliver because He knows all
of us by name and he knows where we live.

David declared he knows my down
sitting and my uprising, he knows, yes he
knows!

Man's delivery has <u>price</u>
limitations: Without a postage stamp the
mail won't be delivered for you must pay

the price---But God deliver salvation without a price or a charge, for it was paid by Jesus, the Lamb of God.

Yes! The Song says…

Jesus! Paid it all

All to Him we owe

Sin had left a crimson stain

But He washed it whiter than snow

"He's An On Time God"

Joseph R. Rogers, Sr., D. Min.

Pastor/Teacher

"The Greatest Come Back"
A Sermon Dr. Joseph R. Rogers, Sr.
For The Greater Philadelphia Church
Raleigh, North Carolina 28703
Theme: Down But Not Out
March 20, 2011

Scripture: "Rejoice not against me, O mine enemy: when I -fall- (mess up), I shall -arise- (recover); when I sit in -darkness-, the LORD shall be a -light (directions)- unto me." **(Micah 7:8)**

Introduction
Today, it is my prayer that this message will be very encouraging and uplifting. It is also my prayer that it gives us the stimuli to know that even though we might get down; but yet there is always room for a comeback.

The text says to our enemies and foes; we make get down but there is one thing for sure, that is, we are never out. Yes we may be...

- Troubled on every side, yet not distressed;
- Perplexed, but not in despair;
- Persecuted, but not forsaken;

- Cast down, but not destroyed;
  but there is always room for a
  comeback.

Yes! We will rise from our temporary
rugged mountains!
Yes! We will arise from our lonesome
valleys!
Yes! We will arise from our
challenges of this life.

How are we sure this will happen,
"when we fall, we shall arise; when we
sit in darkness, the LORD shall be a
light unto us"

What is a comeback? A Comeback is
when your opponents have you outscored
and there appears no chance of you
recovering or winning the game or
contest, but somehow another you
recovery, miraculously, and gain momentum
and end up winners.

That's when the underdogs are become
the Top Dogs.
That's when the losers become
winners.
**That's when those who thought they
were going to win** lose their
momentum and become disorganized.

29

In fact, the ability to comeback is what separates champions from mere competitors. Now we must be aware that every team at some point will fall behind, but only the champions come back and win. Let us look at some examples:

In Super Bowl XXV the Giants trailed the Bills by nine points in the second quarter, 12-3. Although they trailed by more than a touchdown and they made a comeback to win the game.

In Super Bowl XXII, the Washington Redskins trailed the Denver Broncos 10-0 at the start of the second quarter. Washington then scored 35 points in the second quarter to set a Super Bowl record for points in a quarter. Washington won the game 42-10.

As Christians we praise God for his willingness to help us comeback from setbacks and experience life's victories.

Exposition I
This text focuses on the Prophet Micah as he speaks to Israel about its national dilemma. The people were suffering considerable hardship. They are in a depressed condition. All they hear

is bad news about the nation's economy and security.

The nation's enemies **gloats** *(to feel or express smug self-satisfaction about something)* and rejoices at what seems to be helplessness situation, but the Israelites would recover and get back in the game, because they serve a God who knows comebacks.

The Prophet Micah painted a dreary picture for Israel that portrayed them trailing, losing ground, fumbling and making sinful errors that would cause them to fall out of contentions with their foe. However, in the midst of this challenging situation The Prophet offered a word (ray) of hope.

That is, although the situation looked dark and defeat appear imminent, yet The Prophet says in Chapter Seven, Verse eight, *"Rejoice not against me, O mine enemy: when I fall, I shall arise; when I sit in darkness, the LORD shall be a light unto me."*

- Though down, they would recover!
- Though depressed, they would recover!

- Though out of favor, they would recover!

Because, weeping may endure for the night, but joy will come in the morning. No! No weapon that forms itself against us will prosper.

The Prophet Micah made it plain that setbacks because of sin, mistakes, errors and fumbled plays are to be expected. However, God's people should never lose hope because despite of setbacks God will give us the power to make a comeback!

So, therefore, my brothers and sisters if you find yourself today/tonight in the midst of the game of life and it appear as though time is running out; hold fast unto you faith. You can make a comeback!

Again, every one of us will get behind in the game of life. I read somewhat that, *"Live is not fair"*. That simply means that in this life we will have trials and tribulation—but in the midst of them all remember that we are more than conquerors through Him who gives us strength.

The real problem is not that we fall behind, the real problems is how do we respond when we get behind.

- o There is no perfect marriage relationship!
- o There is no perfect financial situation!
- o There is no perfect career pursuit!
- o There is no perfect local church!
- o There is no perfect friendship relationship!

And the sad part of it all is that we fall behind our so called friends or enemies gloat; they **"rejoice"** because we seem **"defeated"**. Speak to our enemies and tell them, *"Rejoice not against me, O mine enemy"*- that means it ain't over until God says it is over.

Yes! We might suffer setbacks but our God assures us that falling the not the end of the book of life, because God also assures that we shall recover and stand again.

Conclusion
So, as I close this message, I am happy to know that God will always come

to our rescue. I will never forsake those who walk in His principles and statues.

Yes! When I fall, I shall arise; when I sit in darkness, the LORD shall be a light unto me." (Micah 7:8) The scoreboard may indicate that I am two or three touchdowns behind with only minutes left to play but I will never lost hope. I might look *confusion, trouble, despaired, depressed and fearful*, but I still have hope. I am about to get my second wind.

Donnie McClurkin wrote a song some time ago, *"We fall down, but we get up."* If anyone judges you when you are down they are making a mistake.
Tell them your present situation is only a comma situation of your life and not a period—you will make a comeback!

Tell them you are on your way back and don't watch your mistakes and errors, watch you make a comeback!

Tell them that you will not allow the arrow by day nor the terror by night to cause you to doubt The Lord--you will make a comeback!

When Bill Clinton made his first run for the Presidency of the United States he lost several key states, he refused to be counted out--"He made a comeback"

When Barack Obama lost a primary or two in his presidential bid, but he refused to be count out—he made a comeback all the way to the White House.

Today, my friends we too can comeback! Every believer, Every Child of God can become a comeback kid. I don't know about you but I'm glad to know that we serve a God that can help us to come back from any challenge or situation. The God of the bible will take our

- ✓ Defeats and turn it into victories;
- ✓ Failures and turn it into successes
- ✓ Misfortunes and turn it into good fortunes;
- ✓ Tragedy's and turn it into opportunities
- ✓ Blunders and turn them into wonders;

This comeback kid, **"Jesus Christ"**

- ➢ He was born in the worse of circumstances and lived in the worst of towns, but he made a comeback!
- ➢ He was put down by the people of his own home town and run down by the leaders of town, but he made a comeback!
- ➢ He had no house or a place to call home, for I heard him say, "Foxes have holes and birds have nests, but the son of man hath no place to lay his head", but he made a comeback!
- ➢ He was lied on in court and falsely accused, but he still made a comeback!
- ➢ He nailed him to an old rugged cross and stuck a spear in his side, but he made a comeback!
- ➢ He was spit on, taunted, and mocked by the Roman Soldier, but he still made a comeback.

At Calvary, the world thought the He was defeated. But early, Sunday morning he arose from the grave with all power in his hands! Jesus Made A Come Back, with all POWER IN HIS HANDS!

He took the **"sting"** out of death!

He took the **"victory"** out of the grave!

And He is coming back again—to gather together His Saints!
"The Greatest Come Back"
Joseph R. Rogers, Sr., D. Min.
Pastor/Teacher

"My Shepherd"

A Sermon By Joseph R. Rogers, Sr.
For The Philadelphia Baptist Church
Raleigh, North Carolina 27603
Theme: Blessed
April 10, 2011

Scripture: "The Lord (Jesus Christ) IS (right now) my Shepherd (guide, outlook, provider) I shall not (will not ever) WANT (be without...the needed necessities) (Psalm 23:1)(Read 23:1-6)

Introduction

My brothers and sisters it is good to know that even in the midst of heartache, pain, or suffering there is a way of escape. The escape vehicle is our Great Shepherd, Jesus Christ.

You see, the Lord Jesus Christ is our "light" in darkness, "shelter" is time of storms, "healing" is times of sickness and "supplier" in times of need.

We have the -assurance- in the Word of God that -He- may now come when we want Him, but He will always be on time. He will *make* our enemies our footstools and never allow them to have victory over His children.

The Twenty-third Psalm is the favorite Psalm of most believers. It is recited at many home goings services and bedsides the beds of sick love one who need the Spirit's intervention.

The Twenty-third Psalm is a favorite Psalm because it is a personal Psalm--the personal pronouns "I", "Me", "My", or "Mine" occur eighteen times (8) in the Psalm's six verses.

It is personal because it does not matter where you are, "The Lord Can Be Your Shepherd". This relationship is not limited to geographical locations, race, economic status, political affiliation, or academic abilities because it is more of a spiritual relationship than natural.

Even though is this text, King David address God as his "Shepherd", there are three (3) primary names for God revealed to us in His Holy Word: **"El"** (Plural: Elohim), **"Adonai"**, and **"Jehovah"**.

**Elohim is used 2,570 times and it refers to God's power, intelligence, and wisdom. (Gen. 1:1, Psalm 19:1) There are four compounds of the name El:

> **El yon**, the strongest strong One.
> (Gen. 14:17-20)
>
> **El Roi**, the strong One Who sees.
> (Gen. 16:13)
>
> **El Shaddai**, the breasted one--comforter, sustainer, and nurturer.
> (Gen. 17:1, Psalm 91:1)
>
> **El Olam**: the everlasting God.
> (Isaiah 40:28-31)

Now, **Adonai**, the second of these titles, means "Master, Lord" (Mal. 1:6). It is the New Testament counterpart of Kurios, "Lord".

Jehovah, the self-existent One, is the God of the Covenant. It is God's most common name--occurring 6,823 times in the Bible. It is the combination of the vowels from **"Adonai"** and **"YHWH",** the verb, "I am" or "to be".

The Jews purposely omitted the vowels from this name for God, YHWH, in order to prevent the profane use of the

Holy Name (Exodus 20:7). Additionally, there are nine (9) combinations of His personal Name, Jehovah, that reveal His nature and character:

Jehovah Rohi:
"The Lord my Shepherd".
Psalm 23:1- "The LORD is my shepherd; I shall not want".

Jehovah Jireh:
"The Lord will provide".
Gensis 22:13-"And Abraham lifted up his eyes, and looked, and behold behind him a ram caught in a thicket by his horns:...14 And Abraham called the name of that place Jehovah jireh: as it is said to this day, In the mount of the LORD it shall be seen".

Exposition I
Jehovah Rapha:
"The Lord our Healer".
Exodus 15:26-"And said, If thou wilt diligently hearken to the voice of the LORD thy God... I will put none of these diseases upon thee, which I have brought uponn the Egyptians: for I am the LORD that healeth thee".

Jehovah Maccaddeschcem:
"The Lord thy Sanctifier".

Exodus 31:13-"Speak thou also unto the children of Israel, saying, Verily my sabbaths ye shall keep: for it is a sign between me and you throughout your generations; that ye may know that I am the LORD that doth sanctify you".

Jehovah Tsidkenu:
"The Lord our Righteousness"
Jeremiah 23:6-"In his days Judah shall be saved, and Israel shall dwell safely: and this is his name whereby he shall be called, THE LORD OUR RIGHTEOUSNESS".

Jehovah Shalom:
"The Lord is Peace"
Judges 6:24-"Then Gideon built an altar there unto the LORD, and called it Jehovahshalom: unto this day it is yet in Ophrah of the Abiezrites".

Jehovah Shammah:
"The Lord who is present"
Ezekekiel 48:35 "...and the name of the city from that day shall be, The LORD is there".

Jehovah Sabaoth:
"The Lord of hosts"
Isaiah 6:3-"Holy, holy, holy, is the LORD of hosts: the whole earth is full of

his glory".

Jehovah Nissi:
"The Lord, my Banner"
Exodus 17:15-"And Moses built an altar, and called the name of it Jehovahnissi":

This Psalm is wonderful, magnificent, and comforting, and I love many of the others also….

Psalm 1—Blessed is the man...

Psalm 15-Who shall abide in thy tabernacle?

Psalm 27-The Lord is my light and my salvation.

Psalm 37-Fret not thyself because of evildoers.

Psalm 121-I will lift mine eyes unto the hills, from whence cometh my help and

Psalm 150-Praise ye the Lord…

But, the text Psalm is my favorite. (Psalm 23)

Exposition I

I love Psalm 23 because it is Personal, Touching, Rewarding and it speaks directly to the -heart- and -soul- of mankind.

1. Because, The LORD is my Shepherd,

I shall not lack any provision in needs of my life.

2. Because, He makes me lie down in green pastures,

I shall not lack nourishment.

3. Because, He leads me beside quiet waters,

I shall not lack rest.

4. Because, He restores my soul,

I shall not lack forgiveness and restoration.

5. Because, He guides me in the paths of righteousness for His name sake,

I shall not lack a right relationship with God.

6. Because, I walk through the valley of the shadow of death, I fear no evil, and
I shall not lack encouragement and hope.

Conclusion

So, as I close this message to day, I am happy to know and to be assured in the Word of God, that, Because The Lord is my Shepherd—everything will be all right!!

7. Because, Thou art with me,

I shall not lack for a constant companion.

8. Because, Thy rod and Thy staff comfort me,

I shall not lack guidance and protection.

9. Because, Thou preparest a table before me in the presence of my enemies, I shall not lack honor and respect.

10. Because, Thou hast anointed my head with oil,

I shall not lack power and authority,

11. Because, My cup runneth over, I shall not lack joy, and abundant life.

12. Because, goodness and mercy shall follow me all the days of my life,

I shall not lack contentment.

13. Because, I dwell in the house of the LORD forever,

I shall not lack assurance of eternal security.

There is none other relationship than there are between the Shepherd and the Sheep. I have be said that the 'Sheep" are without the ability to travel alone.

That is why they need a Shepherd to be their guide!

That is why they need a Shepherd to nourish them!

That is why they need a Shepherd to comfort in tough times!

I am elate and secure in know that, The Lord is our shepherd and we shall not want—Because The Lord Is My Shepherd!

"My Shepherd"
Joseph R. Rogers, Sr., D. Min.
Pastor/Teacher

"Easter: A Time Of Decision"
A Sermon By Dr. Joseph R. Rogers, Sr.
For The Greater Philadelphia Church
Raleigh, North Carolina 27603
Theme: The Resurrection
April 24, 2011

Scripture: "And the Jews' PASSOVER was at hand, and Jesus went up to Jerusalem. Jesus answered and said unto them DESTROY this TEMPLE, and in THREE DAYS I will RAISE it up". (St. John 2:13, 19)

Introduction
What is it that draws more people to church on Easter SundayMore than any other Sunday during the year? The answer is so simple that most of us miss it. Well, "Easter" or "The Resurrection" is a time of decision.

It is a time for many to make a final choice: much like our Savior did: to go all the way with God. Easter has a sense of finality about it. If we go all the way with God, then we, like our Lord, will face crucifixion.

This is not a physical crucifixion, but a spiritual crucifixion. One wherein

you and I die to the FLESH that our
SPIRITUAL MAN might come alive and take
control.

Easter the time of spring; Easter
the time of refreshing; Easter a time of
looking deep within ourselves and
allowing the Spirit of The Lord to RISE
US UP AGAIN A NEW.

Millions will be in churches today,
and they will walk right up to the foot
of the cross and ponder this choice of
whether to continue to die or live; and
sadly most will turn back. WHY?

The Jewish Passover is a time when
the chosen people of God come together
and remember the coming out of Egypt
(bondage) and being liberate in the
wilderness of FREEDOM. It is a time when
they remember the PROCTECTION OF THE
BLOOD SACRIFICE of Jehovah God place over
the doorpost.

It is a wonderful thing to know that
the Lord is always present making
intercession for you. It is a wonderful
thing to know that the Lord will not
leave you in the hands of the enemy. It
is a wonder thing to know that whatever

Satan tries to do to you the Lord is always nigh.

It is DECISION TIME! It is about your DESTINY! It is about where you are going to spend eternity! You see, you cannot say 'Happy EASTER' if you are lost. You see, you cannot say "Happy EASTER" if you know not the SAVIOR.

"Easter A Time Of Decision"

Exposition I

So, why are we here today? Why do we celebrate Easter? What is Easter all about? What does Easter mean to you? Let us see why we come annual to celebrate Easter.

I. Because Easter Is About Life And Death:

Jesus didn't make His choice in the Garden of Gethsemene, butin eternity past. The whole purpose of His life was to come anddie on that cross.

God The Father knew that man was too frail and weak to save himself, so He embodied himself in the sinful flesh to come and die for man. You should be grateful that the Lord looked beyond our 'faults' and delivered base upon our 'needs'.

When do most people make their choice between life & death? Some on their death beds. But sadly, many NEVER do. They don't really take the time to even examine the choice.

They are so busy trying to survive, or so busy enjoying the things of this world. Usually, eternity is the farthest thing from their minds.

The greatest error that man makes is thinking that he canHave life without death! But 'real life' begins at death!! Youdon't live the Christian Life without first dying.

Most people don't want to die a natural death - and many also refuse to die totheir sins, but this brothers and sisters is a great conflict at Easter.

II. Easter Is about A Great Hope:
Hope is an expectation of good new or results. It is a sure longing that some good will happen. It is a desire knowing that the results will be heavenly.

Jesus spoke it in vs.19! Here, He speaks of what mankind hasdreamed could

be true since the beginning of time: that somehow
death could be defeated! And here, HE says that HE can do it!

St John 2:19-"Jesus answered and said unto them, destroy this temple, and in three days I will raise it up".

This 'great hope' is nothing less than a resurrection from the dead. And every single Christian- one who has placed his/hertrust in Jesus Christ for the forgiveness of sins, SHARES THIS HOPE! IT IS OURS! JESUS SAID THAT HE WOULD RAISE US UP TOO!!

You and I cannot defeat death. Jesus has taken the string out of DEATH, the victory from the GRAVE. All Power is in His hand because I removed the keys from Satan.

You see, "My HOPE is built on nothing less but Jesus' blood and righteousness, I dare not trust the sweetest frame, but I wholly learn on Jesus' name.

On Christ The Solid Rock I Stand, All Other Ground Is Sinking Sand".
"Easter: A Time Of Decision"

So, as I close this message there is one more thing that I would like to say concerning this topic and that is...

III. Easter Is About A Great Faith:
Faith that is not wavering. Faith that is steadfast and unmovable.

Faith that is not toss to a fro. But, a FAITH that will weather the storms of live and that will go through any adverse situation.

What is FAITH? The Hebrew Writer Chapter Eleven verse one, says it this way, "Now FAITH is the substance of things hopeth for and the evidence of things not seen".

Verse six says,…"and without FAITH it is IMPOSSIBLE to please him: For he that cometh to Him must believe that he is a rewarder of them that diligently seek him".

My 'Great Hope' is rooted in a 'Great Faith' that is anchored in "Great FACTS". All through His earthly ministry, Jesus always gave FACTS when He asked people to believe something.

He raised the dead, He healed the sick, He fed the crowds, He did many miracles. And when He made this great claim in verse 19, He DEMONSTRATED THAT HE COULD DO IT!

I don't believe in fairy tales. I believe in a FACT that has withstood 2000 years of scrutiny! The conclusion of the facts is that death is NOT the 'final place' or 'state for me'! Where Jesus is now, is where all believers will be on that day when our life on this earth is over.

The Master (Jesus Christ) said that he was going away to prepare a place for us, and that He would come back again to get us—I will be happy!!

It is going to be in a moment, in a twinkling of an eye that the 'dead in Christ' shall rise and those 'who are a live and remain' shall be caught up together to meet Him in the clouds.

In order for Christ to raise us up; then it is without question that He must have resurrection power. This is apparent to all who know Him that His Is The Resurrection and The Life.

If Christ be not risen from the dead himself, he hath not the power to raise us. But, I am happy to announce that the Lord got up early EASTER SUNDAY MORNING with ALL POWER IN HIS HAND. The Power to:

*Take Way The Power of The Grave,
*Remove The String of Death,
*Declaw The Devil Bite,
*Bruised The Devil Head,
*Heal The Sick,
*Deliver The Downtrodden,
*Save The Lost,
*Easy burdens of The Weary,

But, also the Power to Resurrect The Saints,

Easter is about the great choice between 'life' and 'death'. Have you made it? Today can be your resurrection day!! A day that will enable you to say, Happy Easter with joy, surety, and conviction!
"Easter: A Time Of Decision"
Joseph R. Rogers, Sr., D. Min.
Pastor/Teacher

"The Resurrection Power"
A Sermon By Dr. Joseph R. Rogers, Sr.
For The Greater Philadelphia Church
Raleigh, North Carolina 27603
Theme: Power Over Death, Hell & The Grave
April 24, 2011

Scripture: "Jesus said to her, "I am the 'resurrection' and the 'life'; he that believeth in 'Me', though he were dead, yet shall he live. And whosoever 'liveth' and 'believeth' in Me shall NEVER die. Believest thou this?" (St. John 11:25-26)

Introduction
He is risen! He is risen indeed was great comforting new to the following of Jesus Christ! That "is" our joyous confession on this Resurrection Sunday Morning. In fact, that was the confession of the early Christians on "Every Sunday".

You see, the very existence of 'Christian Worship and Fellowship' on Sunday, (the first day of the week), is historical evidence of the Resurrection of Jesus Christ and that He lives today!

For Christians, Sunday is the Lord's Day. And the reason why we 'worship' on Sunday is because our Lord 'rose' from

56

the dead on the 'first day' of the week
and not the 'seventh day'. The seventh
day worship is more Jewish, but the
'first day' worship is Christian.

Even though we 'celebrate' our
Lord's Resurrection in a special way once
a year, "Every Sunday" is Resurrection!
Why? Because this is the day that the
Lord hath made and we will rejoice and be
glad in it.

The Apostle Paul said that without
the 'reality' of the resurrection, our
'preaching' (teaching) was vain and our
'faith' was vain (empty; worthless) If
Jesus Christ did not rise from the dead,
then He was a 'fake', and we would be
fools to follow a death leader and
savior.

If Christ 'is' not whom He said He
was and we are still 'lost' and in our
"sins" and on our way to a devil's
"hell". The Validity of Christianity
rises from the dead would be the biggest
hoax in the world.

Our 'Faith' is based on not only on
the virgin birth, sinless life,
sacrificial death of Jesus, but most
importantly upon his resurrection.

In Romans 1:4-"*And declared to be the Son of God with power, according to the spirit of holiness, by the resurrection from the dead*". Christianity rests and is foundation upon this miracle!

Jesus Christ's Resurrection from the dead is significant for the believer for several important reasons. Those reasons revolve not only around proving the soundness Christianity but also around the Implications of His Resurrection for all humanity.

His resurrection not only says something about Him; it also says something about the possibilities for all of us. The Apostle Paul, writing in Philippians 3:10, virtually shouts the desire of his heart: "*That I may know Him, and the power of His Resurrection.*" (Coming Back From The Dead) (He died, but Rose)

It was Paul's earnest desire to be a '*partaker*' of the Resurrection Power of Jesus Christ. That was one of the deepest desires of his heart. It should be our desire as well.

Exposition I

In the text Scripture John, shares a very important declaration made by Jesus Himself. He declares that He is the Resurrection and the life.

In other words, *He is Resurrection Power*. It is important to note that He did not say that He 'has' resurrection power, but that He "is" The Resurrection Power. He said, "I am the Resurrection and the Life".

Now, this text is center around a conversation Jesus was having with Martha, the sister of Lazarus. For Jesus to come and HEAL him. You see, word had been sent to Jesus Christ while Lazarus was still sick, but Jesus had delayed His coming.

And allow Lazarus to lie in the grave for four days. This would satisfied the Jews belief of body decay! When Jesus arrived on the *'scene'* Martha had rushed out to meet Him. She engaged Him telling Him He was 'too late'.

She said, in verse 21, *"Lord, if You had been here, my brother would not have died."* Jesus attempted to redirect her *'attitude'* from one of 'despair' to one of *'hope'* by saying, in verse 23, *"Your brother shall rise again"*.

Martha, however, assumed Jesus was referring to the *'resurrection of the dead'* on the last day of GRACE when The King of kings would come and rapture the believer in mid air. Jesus is saying, "Lazarus will RISE AGAIN". Why? Because, "I m the Resurrection and the Life". If Jesus is *'The Resurrection and The Life'*: *'He Lives'*, *'We also shall live again.*

Exposition II
A. He Lives:
The first thing we need to see is, Jesus *'is'* the resurrection and it means that He lives. The resurrection power of Jesus Christ means that the *'chains of death'* and the *'chillness of grave'* could not hold Him hostage.

Now let us be real Jesus had to die—that was the penatly for sin! Even though Christ die for the sins of the world—physically, yet because He is God, death was not able to conqueror Him. "For He arose from the dead".

He *'broke'* the chains of death. He *'defeated'* the power of hell. From that *'tomb'* He came forth in *'victory'* and *'in

power'. Because Christ is alive, He is
the victorious, He is the King of Kings
and Lord of Lords. There were at least
ten appearances of Christ after rising
for the dead.

This proves that He did not remain
in the grave as: Daddy Grace, Father
Divine, Jim Jones, Joseph Smith, Elijah
M. etc..

B. We Live:

Not only does Resurrection Power
mean that 'Jesus Lives', it also means
that 'We live'. Jesus said, *"I am the
'resurrection' and the 'life'; 'he' (you
and I) that believeth in 'Me', though he
were dead, yet shall he live."*

The truth of the 'Power of Christ's
Resurrection' is that *'believers'* will
also *'rise again'*. Jesus said that even
if we die (In Him), we will live
'eternal' with Him.

In other words, just as He came
forth from that grave, so also will we
come forth from our graves in that great
resurrection morning. And, because He is
the resurrection, those of us who are in
Him shall come forth as well.

Yes! Because He (Jesus) lives I can face tomorrow, because He lives all fear is gone. Notice the qualification put on this: For us to be partakers of this promise, we must be 'believers' in Him.

Jesus said, "*He who believes in Me shall never die.*" Only those who are believers in the Lord Jesus Christ shall 'enjoy' the 'full force' of this promise. The Resurrection Power of Christ is at work in those who put their faith in Him.

Conclusion

So, as I close this text brothers and sisters there is one more thing that I would like to say concerning this topic and that is:

C. We Live Forever:

The Resurrection Power of Jesus means that *'He lives'*; it means that *'we live'*; but it also means that 'we live forever'. The text says, "*And whosoever liveth and believeth in Me (Jesus) shall never die*". Not only did Jesus promise the believer that he would be *'raised from the dead'*, Jesus promises all of us that we shall *'never die again'*.

Eternal life means that we will live forever in the 'joys of heaven'.

- Golden Streets
- Tree With Healing Leaves
- River Clear As Crystal
- No More Tears
- No More Pain
- No More Dying

In this position, We will then be able to enjoy the song:

When we've been there ten-thousand years, Bright shining as the sun, We've no less days to sing God's praise, Than when we first begun.

Yes! We will in joyous bliss forever. We will live in His presence forever to enjoy the glories of the Lord.

Yes! We will be in joyous bliss forever. We will exclaim forever and ever howdy howdy and never good-by.

Yes! We will be in joyous bliss forever. We will experience no more pain from the wicked and we will be in eternal rest.

It will be something like this:

*What a day that will be,
*When my Jesus I shall see,
*When I look upon His face,
*The one who saved me by His grace,
*When He takes me by the hand,
*And leads me to the promised land,
*What a day, glorious day, that will be.

Our destiny in Christ is secure forever. Because, Jesus has risen from the dead, He is 'alive' today to 'live' within each believer. I am glad that the God I 'know' and 'serve' is not on the 'CROSS', neither in the 'GRAVE', but He sit at the right hand of The Father as my Great High Priest making intercession every moment for me.

Yes! He Arose, He Arose, He Arose Form The Dead. And that 'quicken power' still has power. Do you have Him? Do you know Him? It's Wonder Working POWER OF THE LORD!

"The Resurrection Power"
Joseph R. Rogers, Sr., D. Min.
Pastor/Teacher

Behold, The King Cometh"
A sermon By Dr. Joseph R. Rogers, Sr.
For The Greater Philadelphia Church, Inc
Raleigh, North Carolina 27603
Theme: Jesus' Triumphant Entry
April 17, 2011

Scripture: "…when they heard that "Jesus" was coming to Jerusalem, Took branches of -Psalm Trees- and went forth to meet Him, and cried, HOSANA: (Save Now-Ps.118) Blessed is King of Israel that cometh in the name of the Lord". (St John 12:12b, 13) (Also Read Zechariah 9:9)

Introduction

My brothers and sister as we come today to celebrate was is known as, "Psalm Sunday" and prelude to the "crucifixion" of the spotless Lamb, Jesus we should be overjoyed to know the God love us so much that I was willing to give the inevitable to saved us—His Life.

The crowd on "Psalm Sunday" said, "Blessed is King of the Jews; while just six days later the same crowd said, "Crucify" him. What a difference a few day can make. Well, always remember that those who "Hail" you on one that will "critical" of you on the next day.

My brothers and sisters ever since the fall of man in the Garden of Eden, God has been moving humanity toward the Day of Redemption for his humanity.

The perfect fellowship that existed doing man's Dispensation of Innocence was broken when Adam & Eve moved contrary to God's command-eating the forbidden tree!

Since that act the Lord had offered many ways to bring man back into perfect fellowship: He offered The Law, The Judges, The Kings and The Prophet. But, done work to God satisfaction.

The Perfect Substitute for the sins of the world never came through the blood of Lambs, Goats, or Doves. Nor it come through personalities-Moses, Joshua, David, Isaiah, Ezekiel nor John The Baptist.

My brothers and sisters the only "Lamb" that God would receive had to be a "Perfect Lamb", a lamb without spot or wrinkle-- Lord Jesus Christ.

God prophesied to His Chose People (The Jews) that a Son would be born and that a Child would be give— and His name would be called Emmanuel (God with us). Yes! He would be called, Wonderful, The

Mighty God, The Everlasting Father, The Prince of Peace, The Lilly of the Valley and The Bright and Morning Star. Yes! It is without a doubt He came.

God spoke through the Prophet Zechariah prophecy was which states: "Rejoice greatly, O Daughter of Zion! Shout, Daughter of Jerusalem! See your – King- cometh to you, righteous and having SALVATION, gentle and riding on a donkey, on a colt, the foal of a donkey". (Zech. 9:9)

When Jesus entered Jerusalem he clearly understood the mood of the people, the needs of the people and who the people were in expectation of–A King!

Yes! This event involves some "low's" as well as some "high's".
Yes, Jesus "suffered", but yet in that suffering would:

Pay the penalty for sin (death).
Open the door for fellowship (salvation)
Take away the sting of dearth and snatch away the power of the grave.

Aren't you glad that Jesus The King came to bring prove away for you out of darkness into the marvelous light of His goodness and righteousness?

Exposition I
I. How Would The King Come:
In the minds of the Jews, He should "burst" on the scene and deliver them for the bondage of the Roman government. In the mind of the Jews, Jesus should "burst" on the scene and establish his Kingdom here on earth.

But, He came "low" and "meek" as a lamb led dumb to the slaughter. He came with "humility' and "love". He came "willing" and "able" to get the job do. He came in obedience to his father.

II. For What Purpose Did Jesus Come:
It is obvious that Jesus came to bring "DELIVERANCE". It is obvious that Jesus came to bring "HEALING". It is obvious that Jesus came to bring "POWER"! Yes! He came to crush the head of the enemy.

Yes! He came to -die- for sin:
"For the wages of sin is death, but the gift of God is eternal life."

Yes! He came to -draw- men unto himself:

"For if I, if I be lifted up from the earth, I will draw all men unto Me".

II. What Did Jesus Promise At His Coming:
It is obvious that the Lord Promise us a building (house) not make by hands, eternal in the heavens. He promised us "HOPE": The kind of HOPE that would deliver us from whatever grip the Devil had on us.

Yes! He promised us a Revelation (Insights)
Yes! He promised us a Release (Penalty of Sin)
Yes! He promised us a Rescue (Strongholds of Satan)

The King Cometh! The King Has Come! The King Will Come Again. To bring Joy, Hope, Peace and Love to all who would accept His gift.

Conclusion
So, in closing I am glad to be a part of another "Psalm Sunday's Celebration", but I am must grateful to personally know the "King" of Psalm Sunday—Jesus Christ!

Because of God's -intervention- and the Son's obedience, you and I have -VICTORY- through the Name of Jesus. You see, the devil thought he was -in control-, but we know that everything was I the hands of Him who is able to still the water and calm the seas.

The text says, ""…when they -heard- that Jesus was coming to Jerusalem, Took - branches- of Psalm Trees and went forth to met Him, and cried, HOSANA: (Save Now!) Blessed is King of Israel that cometh in the name of the Lord".

You see, they people were overjoyed; for their King was in the House to relieve them of their oppression and torment. And they began to show their joy by spreading branches of Palm Trees and shout, "Hosanna"-Save Now!

You see, the first time Jesus came, He was riding on the foal of a donkey.

But, the second time Jesus comes, He will come riding upon the clouds.

You see, the first time Jesus came, He came subject somewhat to the hands of the Devil.

But, the second time Jesus comes, He will come and once and for all conquer the forces of the Devil.

You see, the first time Jesus came, He came to be humiliated and crucified.

But, the second time Jesus comes, He will come to destroy the works of the Devil.

You see, the first time Jesus came, He came as a lamb to the slaughter.

But the second time Jesus comes, He will come as King of kings and Lord of lord.

You see, the first time Jesus came, He was considered a criminal and judged by Pilate.

But the second time Jesus comes, He will come as The Righteous Judge and He will judge Pilate.

I am happy to know that Jesus came - first- time, but I am overjoyed to know that he coming the -second- time.

When He comes the second time, we will be able to "sup" with Him and enjoy His "fellowship" forever!

I know that when He comes the second time, everything will be alright.

I know that when He comes the second time, there will be no more pain, heartache, disappointment.

I know that when He comes the second time, we shall all gather at the River and drink and never thirst again.

"Behold, The King Cometh"
Joseph R. Rogers, Sr., D. Min.
Pastor/Teacher

"Without The Lord We Can Do Nothing"
A Sermon By Dr. Joseph R. Rogers, Sr.
For the Philadelphia Baptist Church
Raleigh, North Carolina 27603
Theme: We Need The Lord

Scripture: "So Christ was once offered to bear the sins of many; and unto them that look for Him shall he appear the 'second time' without sin unto salvation".
(Hebrews 9:28)

Introduction
We live in a day where there are some physical things that many people just feel like they cannot be without and yet do not look at spiritual things in the same light.

Many feel they cannot do without riches. It is no sin to have a great deal of material possessions, but sin comes in the picture when material possessions have hold of us.

Some folks get obsessed with the thoughts of getting rich. Riches can lead to many things such as pride, forgetting God, denying God, forsaking God, rebelling against God, rejecting Christ (as the rich young ruler), self sufficiency, worry, violence, oppression, fraud and even sensual indulgence.

The Lord Jesus Christ summarized it well when He said, "Life consisteth not in the abundance of things a man possesseth." Jesus says in those words, "Do not build your life around things." We should build our lives around the person of the Lord Jesus Christ.

Riches do not gain for us real prosperity, they certainly cannot redeem the soul, and they cannot deliver in the day of God's wrath. That is why the songwriter said, "Take the whole world but give me Jesus." There are those who feel like they cannot do without worldly fame.

It does not matter if you name is not written on the billboards in this world; God has promised us a new name written down in glory.

It does not matter how many people know you in this world, as long as the Lord know you and you identify as one of His own.

Fame is one of those fleeting things. It may be here today and gone tomorrow. On the other hand, the things of God are invisible, but are eternal.

The Lord has instructed us to build our houses (lives) not upon things that are weak—that is houses of sand.

Exposition I
We need to build upon things that are everlasting and hold to God's unchanging hand. Let's look together for a few minutes today/tonight at some of the **"withouts"** of the Bible.

I. WITHOUT THE SHEDDING OF BLOOD THERE IS NO REMISSION:
Hebrews 9:22-"And almost all things are by the law purged with blood; and without shedding of blood is no remission."

The same Greek NT word for "remission" is translated several times "forgiveness" in the New Testament.

A. Remission is through the riches of His grace.
Ephesians 1:7-"In whom we have redemption through his blood, the forgiveness of sins, according to the riches of his grace;'

B. Remission is through His name.
Acts 10:43-"To him give all the prophets witness, that through his name, whosoever believeth in him shall receive remission of sins".

Remember, my brothers and sisters:

- o Baptism does not save you.
- o Clean Living will not save you.
- o Doing Good will not save you.
- o Joining The Church will not save you.
- o Trying To Keep The Ten Commandments will not save you.

You must have the blood of Christ applied to the soul. "For without the shedding of blood, there is no remission (or forgive-ness)." (Hebrews 9:22).

II. WITHOUT "FAITH" WE CANNOT PLEASE GOD:
Hebrews 11:6-"But without faith [it is] impossible to please [him]: for he that cometh to God must believe that he is, and [that] he is a rewarder of them that diligently seek him.

All of Hebrews 11 is a divine
testimony of lives who pleased God
because they possessed faith. Why can we
not please God except by faith?
**A. Faith please God because it
brings "access" to Him.**
When the jail house at Philippi
collapsed, the jailer went to Paul and
Silas and cried out, "Sirs, what must I
do to be saved? They said to him,
"Believe on the Lord Jesus Christ and
thou shalt be saved."

**B. Faith pleases God because it will
result in the "right kind of life".**
The premise of the entire Book of
James is that saving faith will produce
the right kind of works in a persons
life. We want to do what is right because
of faith being present in our lives.

St. Luke 6:43-"For a good tree
bringeth not forth corrupt fruit; neither
doth a corrupt tree bring forth good
fruit".

James 2:18-"Yea, a man may say, Thou
hast faith, and I have works: shew me thy
faith without thy works, and I will shew
thee my faith by my works."

III. WITHOUT "HOLINESS" NO MAN CAN SEE GOD

Hebrews 12:14-"Follow peace with all [men], and holiness, without which no man shall see the Lord:

There are basically two types of holiness: **"Positional Holiness"** has to do with the time we are saved.

2 Corinthians 5:21-"For he hath made him [to be] sin for us, who knew no sin; that we might be made the righteousness of God in him."

"Practical Holiness" has to do with our lives after we are saved.

I **John 3:9** says if we are born of God, we cannot "commit" or practice sin as a habit. Paraphrased it means you are going to want to live holy once you have been made holy.

IV. WITHOUT "KNOWLEDGE" WE HASTEN ON INTO SIN:

Proverbs 19:2-"Also, [that] the soul [be] without knowledge, [it is] not good; and he that hasteth with [his] feet sinneth.

The Prophet Hosea say, "For my people err, for the lack of knowledge".

V. WITHOUT "CONFIDENCE" WE WOULD BE FILLED WITH FEAR
St. Luke 1:74 "That he would grant unto us, that we being delivered out of the hand of our enemies might serve him without fear"

VI. WITHOUT "CHASTISEMENT", THERE PROOF LACKING OF YOUR SONSHIP
Hebrews 12:8-"But if ye be without chastisement, whereof all are partakers, then are ye bastards, and not sons."

Conclusion
So, as I close this message, I hope that you now have a better understanding of the things you and I cannot do without. Without…

THE **"SHEDDING OF BLOOD"** THERE IS NO REMISSION.

"FAITH" WE CANNOT PLEASE GOD.

"HOLINESS" NO MAN CAN SEE GOD.

"KNOWLEDGE" WE HASTEN ON INTO SIN.

"CONFIDENCE" WE WOULD BE FILLED WITH FEAR.

"CHASTISEMENT", THERE PROOF LACKING OF YOUR SONSHIP

"Without The Lord We Can Do Nothing"
Joseph R. Rogers, Sr., D. Min.
Pastor/Teacher

II. The Author's Contact Information and Other Works

A. Mailing Address:

1313 Ujamaa Drive, Raleigh, NC 27610

Phone Nos.

(919) 208-0200,

(919) 829-7179

B. Email Address:

jroger3420@aol.com,

jrrphila1428@aol.com

C. Websites:

http://gpcminc.cwwsites.com, lulu.com,

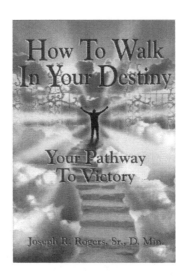

My Role As An Associate Minister
Servants Of God And The Senior Pastor's Armor Bearers

Dr. Joseph R. Rogers, Sr.

Christian Discipleship And The Holy Spirit
Equipping And Empowering For Kingdom Building

Dr. Joseph R Rogers Sr.

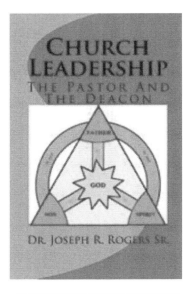

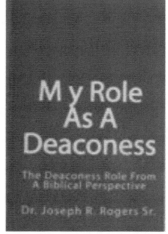

(There Is A Series of 1-18)

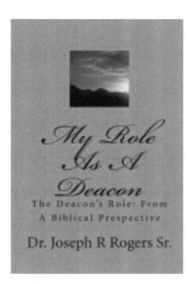

My Role
As A
Deacon
The Deacon's Role: From
A Biblical Prespective

Dr. Joseph R Rogers Sr.

HOW TO STUDY
THE BIBLE (A
STUDY SERIES)
APPLYING THE PROPER
METHODS FOR STUDYING AND
UNDERSTANDING THE SCRIPTURES

DR. JOSEPH R. ROGERS SR.

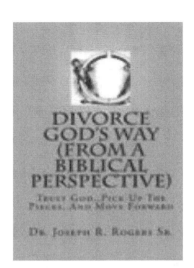

RENEWING YOUR
MIND: SPIRITUAL
INVENTORY

Dr. Joseph R. Rogers, Sr.

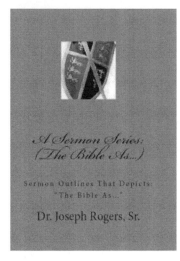

A Sermon Series:
(The Bible As...)

Sermon Outlines That Depicts:
"The Bible As..."

Dr. Joseph Rogers, Sr.

IIII. Notes

Notes Cont.

7977300R0

Made in the USA
Charleston, SC
27 April 2011